A-Z MINDFUL ME

by Lani Gerszonovicz

Copyright Disclaimer
Copyright © 2022 Lani Gerszonovicz (text), All Rights Reserved.
Copyright © 2022 A-Z Mindfulness LLC (text), All Rights Reserved.
Copyright © 2022 A-Z Mindfulness LLC (illustrations), All Rights Reserved.

Without limiting the rights of the copyrights named above, no part of this book may be reproduced, stored in or introduced into a retrieval system or transmitted, in any form or by any means (electronic, mechanical, photocopying, recording, or otherwise, without the prior express written permission from the copyright owners and publisher listed.
Published by
A-Z Mindfulness, LLC
www.a-zmindfulness.com
ISBN 978-1-7331413-1-4 (bound)

With love, light and gratitude for my family, friends, teachers, students; and to life for presenting many opportunities to practice living mindfully.

This collection of mindfulness practices is to be enjoyed at your own pace. Experience one at a time in random order, treat yourself to several activities in one sitting or take a 26-day mindfulness challenge by practicing one each day in consecutive order until completion. Trust your inner-guide and have fun with the present of presence!

AWARENESS grows as you slowly breathe to relax your body and feel at ease.

Focus on what you see; look around name colors, c o u n t 1 - 2 - 3.

Pay attention to sounds you hear; notice if noise seems far away or near.

When you listen to all that sound, is what you're hearing quiet or loud?

Focus on slow breath in and out; calms us down without a doubt.

Breathe in deeply, count 1-2-3; fill up like a balloon it's easy you'll see.

Blow out slowly through open lips; body Awareness feel it down in your hips.

Notice if your body feels heavy or light, or maybe now it feels just right.

Does your body tilt left or right, or is it centered like a tree reaching great height?

When mad or sad don't push away, all feelings come and go and never stay.

Awareness welcomes all parts of ME, feeling best when happy, healthy and free!

BEE BUZZING connects body, breath and mind so peace and clarity you will find.

Breathe in deeply, it's easy to do; hum out with lips closed for five seconds or a few.

Close your eyes and buzz like a bee; vibrate your body to set your mind free.

Buzz vibration tickles your chest; stop and be still take a five second rest.

Practice buzzing long and loud, drowning out all other sound.

Buzz again, look within not around; then stop, be quiet! Do you hear any sound?

Bee Buzzing vibrates muscle, bone, and cell; feel more energized, balanced and well.

CLOUD calms the mind to create inner space when thoughts race all over the place.

Notice a thought and put it in a bubble; a trick, like magic to release mind trouble.

Close your eyes and put a thought in a Cloud; take a deep breath then blow out loud.

Breath like wind blows thoughts away; choose any thoughts that you want to stay.

Thoughts clutter up an open mind; release these thoughts and peace you will find.

When feeling down and need a lift, welcome peace of mind like a precious gift.

Messy thoughts grow just like weeds; put them up in a Cloud, then plant fresh seeds.

Growing good thoughts is ever so sweet; blow away negativity to enjoy this treat.

Breath and Cloud are superpowers; a clear mind is a gift, even better than flowers!

DIRECTOR chooses a story to see, with a clear picture in mind of who and what to be.

What do you do that's loads of fun? Now see yourself doing it, like it's already done.

Name a thing that you are good at; like singing, dancing or playing with a ball or cat.

Do you like to color or bake; what activity is such fun that you don't take a break?

How do you feel when you run, skip or climb; is it possible to have fun all the time?

Maybe you play music or write a book; or do you prefer to read, build, or cook?

Whatever it is that you do best, Director sees it clearly while awake or at rest.

Direct yourself as a superstar, knowing in your heart that you will go far.

The mind is such a powerful tool; Director of your thoughts is a feel-good rule.

ENERGY grows when we focus and breathe, encouraging negative feelings to leave.

Energy is everywhere big and small, inside and around us one and all.

Trust the message that Energy sends; use it wisely when choosing your friends.

Clear negative Energy away; use breath, meditation, movement, or sway.

Clap hands while counting 1-2-3; be still, palms open, let Energy be.

Now practice sitting up real tall and imagine you're playing with an Energy ball.

Move hands back and forth real slow, without letting your focus on Energy go.

Feel this energetic magnetic pull; let body, mind and spirit grow ever so full.

Place your hands at your heart center; feel good Energy grow and enter.

An important message all hearts long to hear; you are special and loved my dear!

Love is the greatest Energy on earth; it grows stronger each day, right from birth.

FIRE BREATH quickly builds up heat to warm the body from head down to feet.

Fire Breath heats up the body from within; burning off negativity, let's begin.

Breathe in and out fast, panting like a dog; then rest, lay down, be still like a log.

Hold your body very still; feel your feelings and connect with free-will.

With a hand on belly, pant in and out; move it back and forth to build energy clout.

Stop panting, be still, notice how you feel; to support your body and mind to heal.

Fire Breath moves quickly through mouth or nose; try it while doing a yoga pose.

With regular practice of breath of fire, mood and energy lift higher and higher!

GRATITUDE says thanks out loud or in head, do it while awake or before going to bed.

Thank all people, places and things, a fast path to Gratitude and happiness it brings.

For all the people who love you most; to family and friends-let's make a toast!

Be grateful for what they say and do, love grows knowing what they mean to you.

Be thankful when you laugh and play; connect with moments of joy each day!

Are you thankful for people who cook, or do you feel grateful while reading a book?

When you want to feel safe and snug, imagine your family giving you a big hug.

Grateful for school, friends, and a home, and even for time that is spent alone.

Gratitude for food, books, and toys; a full belly and playing are wonderful joys.

I am thankful that I am me; special, loved and feeling ever so free.

Who are you grateful for and why? A Gratitude parade lets good feelings march by.

HAPPY HEALTHY repeat these words in your head, until believing what is being said.

Happy and healthy focus as you say, to attract these feelings each and every day.

Say these words together with me, "I am happy, I am healthy" and so it will be.

Repeat these words until you believe, get energy flowing so you will receive.

Say positive words to the people you love; give this gift to lift mood and spirit above.

To someone special repeat with me, "Be happy and healthy" so that it will be.

Match action with words and do as you say; to be happy and healthy in every way.

Choose how you act and the words you speak, if Happy Healthy is what you seek.

Happy Healthy vibes to others and self, taps into the source of goodness and health!

IMAGINE a place that's peaceful and free; believe it wholeheartedly so that it will be.

Imagine your very own special place, where you do fun things like running a race.

Think about a bright blue sky and sun; Imagine swimming or fishing, oh what fun!

In your mind see a shady nook; where you curl up with your favorite book.

Breathe in and Imagine ocean scent in air; blow out a breeze that moves your hair.

Imagine wind swaying through the trees; feel happy, peaceful, while being at ease.

Imagine feet sinking into warm sand, strolling along with a loved one hand-in-hand.

Imagine feeling happy and proud; in this special place to play or sing out-loud.

Imagine a place that's special to you, doing fun things that you love to do.

When you want to feel safe and secure; Imagine this place to feel better for sure!

JIGGLE JAM so your body moves and shakes; jiggle and jump until you feel awake.

Take a deep breath right into your belly; blow it out slowly and jiggle like jelly.

Move while stretching fingers and toes; can you even wiggle your little nose?

Let's try together this joyful trick, to get your whole body moving real quick.

Stretch your arms up high overhead, then shake and jump to get out the lead.

Jiggle your legs you're almost ready; wiggle and shake til they feel like spaghetti.

Hop up and down, leap for the sky; get into the rhythm, feel like you can fly.

Move, jump, and Jiggle Jam up and down; stop into stillness, feet settle in ground.

Take a big breath to fill your belly, then let it out slowly and set like jelly.

Can you feel good energy flow? Jiggle Jam try it and let all tension go!

KINDNESS given to others or self, is a superpower to attract happiness and health.

Be kind in action, thought and word; a shift in attitude lets truth be heard.

Whether kind to self or others in need, acts of Kindness are valued indeed.

Kindness is a great gift to send; to yourself, or family or even a friend.

Speak to yourself and kindly say, "I love myself, I'm special" at least once a day.

Kindness begins being good to self; then spread it to others as a gift of great wealth.

Be kind with what you do or say; Kindness like magic brightens up each day.

Share with others, help out and give hugs; be kind to all nature, even the bugs.

Whether playing with friends or alone for a rest, be kind and always do your best!

LION'S BREATH will let go of stress; release tense feelings when under duress.

Breathe in like a lion strong and proud; breathe out with a gentle roar out loud.

Sounds like "haaa" a quiet roar, Lion's Breath lets your energy soar.

Breathe in deeply so body expands; stretch fingers like claws which are your hands.

Open your mouth, let a mindful roar out; to release stress, tension, and anger about.

Breathe in, you know just what to do; Lion's Breath release to become the best you.

Lion is a strong confident king; with practice you can do most anything!

MINDFUL MOVEMENT lets body and breath move; do this now to get into the groove.

Stretch your arms up and reach for the sky; pretend like you are waving goodbye.

Now fold over and reach for the ground, do this quietly without making a sound.

Take a deep breath and stretch up high, imagine you're a superhero who can fly.

Reach up more and breath out slow; connect to mindful movement here we go.

Now breathe in deeply and reach up higher, pretend that you're a super flyer.

Breathe out while reaching hands for floor; body and breath as one lets energy soar.

Stretch arms up as high as they go; breathe while swaying side to side real slow.

Rest arms by sides, stand tall like a tree; this is how we start to move mindfully.

Focus on motion and being still; Mindful Movement recharges so energy tank fills.

NOTE TO SELF is a kind letter; write loving words and you will feel better.

Powerful words written just for you, bring comfort or joy when feeling blue.

What does your heart most want to hear? Put it down on paper to make it clear.

Write down what your head wants to hear; to comfort self and soothe away fear.

List emotions that you wish to receive; flowing from your heart until you believe.

Say to yourself, "I am strong and smart," kind self-talk is a good place to start.

Write down, "I feel safe and secure," like magnets we attract what we think for sure.

Express fears and let negativity go; a clear mind guides like a compass you know.

Note to Self so mood and energy rise; be your own best friend is both good and wise.

Use kind words in your Note to Self; to attract abundance and create good health.

Note to Self is a wonderful gift, through self-love and kindness mood and energy lift!

OCEAN BREATH gently soothes the soul; breathe in, then out, say "haaa," let's roll.

Breathe in deeply until belly is full; say "haaa" while hearing the ocean pull.

Breathe in slowly, it's the craze; breathe out saying "haaa," to sound like a wave.

Breathe in, lift hands up super high; roll down like a wave, breathe out with a sigh.

Ocean Breath, do it now with closed eyes; breathe in and feel a big wave rise.

Open your mouth, let breath out slow; Ocean Breath soothes, here we go!

Breathe in, hands high, do your best; Ocean Breath out, hands lower and take a rest.

Motion of the ocean will ebb and flow; Ocean Breath is great to let all tension go.

PATTING your body is a gift of self-care; be kind, gentle and loving, not hurting a hair.

Pat each body part for a count of five; make your body feel awake and alive.

Use your hands to pat your thighs, sounds like thunder in the skies.

Begin to lightly pat your belly, in a clockwise circle until it jiggles like jelly.

Take hands up to gently pat your chest, knowing that you are doing your best.

Patting your body lets energy flow; feel more energized and ready to go.

Fingertips lightly Patting your face; move around eyes, cheeks, lips-there's no race.

Pat fingers gently on your neck and head; stop and be still like you're going to bed.

Patting yourself is a gentle massage; self-care a gift better than a flower corsage.

QUEEN SNAKE breath is a tool, to release hot emotions so mind and body feel cool.

Through teeth, hiss out just like a snake; improve your focus, feel more awake.

Pay attention to the long hissing sound; stop, be quiet until peace of mind is found!

Focus on the sound of this long, loud hiss, leads to inner-calm, peace and bliss.

Shape your lips like a tiny "O," then sip in cool air for a slow, deep flow.

As the air travels into mouth, throat, and lungs; feel cool sensation tickling tongues.

Queen Snake hiss out super slow; to fully let stress and worry go.

Queen Snake notice what you feel and hear, to let hot emotions settle and clear.

RELAXATION is a healthier choice than a shout; to let worries, fears, and stress out.

Relax, let go, become self-aware; grow peace and love through precious self-care!

Breathe deeply with awareness down in your toes, then fully relax even your nose.

Connect with body and breath as one; calms and relaxes, for good, grounded fun.

With each breath relax a body part, to ease the mind and soothe your heart.

Relax, close eyes, body is still; Relaxation restores peace of mind and free-will.

Breathe in deeply as you say in your mind, "Relax body, it's time to be self-kind."

Breathe out, let every bit of stress go; a healing practice, you now surely know.

Relaxation slow down and take a rest; rejuvenate self to feel your best.

SQUEEZE RELEASE muscles to make inner space; reset the body to its happy place.

Squeeze Release all tension away; mind and body relax, then peace will stay.

Squeeze every muscle, scrunch up tight; connect with your body feels so right.

Release all muscles and whoosh out a sigh; let tension go to lift mood up high.

Face, hands, and toes squeeze and scrunch; release and feel better by a whole bunch.

Practice, try it, Squeeze Release; feel calm and connect with your inner-peace.

TAKE 5 because sometimes we need a break; take 5 seconds to feel more awake.

Breathe in slowly, count 1-2-3-4-5; feel calm, connected, and super alive.

Hold the breath in as you recount; try 5 seconds or a shorter or longer amount.

Let breath go out with a count to match; recharge yourself and feel more attached.

Do what feels just right for you; Take 5 breathing leaves you feeling brand new.

Try Take 5 breath when you need a rest and put this mindful tool to the test.

Recharge and use a Take 5 break; to reset and center when a lot is at stake.

UNICORN magic so mind, body, and breath link; free up space to clearly think.
Unicorn and breath are magical things; improve self-awareness and focus it brings.
Hands together, lift thumbs to brow; slide hands to heart center, try this now!
Try again, add "haaa" sound like the ocean; listen while hands move in slow motion.
Practice "haaa" while breathing in and out; calms mind and body whenever in doubt.
Unicorn flowing like a magical wave; drop in and focus to feel calm and brave.

VISION with focus so head and heart believe; lay a clear path so you will achieve.

Clearly see who you plan to become; Vision grows confidence so it can be done.

Picture a life you most want to live, a precious gift to self that only you can give.

See this Vision of your future self, who is happy, healthy and enjoying great wealth.

With family at home or friends who are cool, a clear Vision in mind is a winning rule.

Picture your future with ease and grace will put a big smile on your face.

Release any thoughts that hold you back; negativity stops Vision right in its track.

Visualize yourself as a superstar; with clear, focused Vison trust that you will go far.

Turn the noise of mind chatter down; feel like royalty wearing a crown.

Create a clear and positive Vision, a path to success with the greatest precision.

WATER like a mind that is calm and clear, or when cluttered, chaotic and full of fear.

Thoughts like rocks take up space and make ripples that disturb a peaceful place.

Close eyes, see Water calm and still; to restore peaceful feelings and raise good will.

Water so clear, deep, and blue; lift away heaviness like fresh morning dew.

Breathe deep when thoughts feel a mess, to lighten the load and remove any stress.

Watch messy thoughts float away; calm, clear Water is a safe place to stay.

X-TRAORDINARY YOU so special and unique, thrive when quiets the inner critique.

Arms cross like an X and give self a hug; until body feels snug, like a bug in a rug.

Close your eyes, send peace, self-kindness, and love; to lift your mood high above.

X-traordinary YOU simply the best; similar to many, but not exactly like the rest.

Remember a time when you felt proud; turn the volume up so this thought gets loud.

What makes you special in action or look? Become like a superhero in a book.

What do you do that's kind to others? Treat all people nicely, as sisters and brothers.

YELLOW MELLOW connect with radiant light; to self-soothe and feel shiny and bright.

Warm, golden light shines down to guide; awaken calm, safe feelings inside.

Yellow Mellow light shining on your head, soothes and protects without a word said.

Imagine gooey honey dripping down muscle and bone; feel connected, never alone.

Yellow Mellow glows from head down to feet; stop to notice your own heartbeat.

Light rises up, swirling around; connect with sunshine while feeling the ground.

Golden light protects just like a cocoon; imagine floating just like a balloon.

Yellow Mellow laser-like attention is a healing practice surely worth a mention.

ZEN "I AM" the words that I hear, when spoken aloud or whispered in ear.

Zen I Am words to self-express, peace and clarity when the mind seems a mess.

Say a kind word for each alphabet letter; focus this way will make you feel better.

Zen I am Aware, Brave, Calm, Divine, Energy; words have power to set the mind free.

Focus, Grateful, Happy, Imagine, Joy; this practice is fun like playing with a toy.

Kind, Love, Mindful, Nice, Open, Play; like beautiful music, listen today.

Zen I am Quiet, Real, Smart, Tuned-in and Unique; words to quiet my inner critique.

Vibrant, Wise, X-traordinary, Young and Zen; repeat positive words again and again.

Zen I am improving focus, just like magic without hocus pocus.

ABOUT AUTHOR

At age 8, Lani practiced her first mindful breath which sparked a life-long journey of self-discovery. She began her daily mindfulness practice as a young mom. Her passion for educating others was ignited when her elementary aged son suffered anxiety and sleep issues. Lani would comfort him while practicing slow, deep belly breaths together until he learned to self-soothe, relax, and more easily fall asleep. Since 2004, Lani has taught yoga and mindfulness to thousands of students at schools, libraries, sport fields, and in private sessions. Her commitment is to empower each and every student with mindfulness strategies to awaken awareness, kindness, and compassion; creating the potential to self-regulate emotions and better navigate our challenging world.

Lani enjoys living mindfully. Whether hiking, dancing, biking, reading, listening to music, practicing yoga, meditating, or teaching mindfulness, Lani feels best when being fully aware and present. Practicing mindfulness has opened Lani to increased patience and greater joy, while creating a deeper connection to herself, family, friends, and nature.

Being bombarded with information often leaves us feeling distracted, exhausted, anxious, or depressed. Lani's students of yoga and mindfulness consistently requested tools to use outside of class to feel as attentive and peaceful as they felt in class so they could gain benefit and share with their loved ones. This led to the creation of A-Z Mindfulness and her first book *Mindful Students- Social and Emotional Learning in the Classroom and Beyond*. These 26 empowering tools were chosen because they can be practiced almost anywhere, are engaging and easy to learn. Further, they encourage awareness of oneself and the environment and are valuable tools to better navigate growth and development.

Lani's hometown and residence for over 40 years is Highland Park, IL where the incident on July 4, 2022 has forever changed us. We are facing a mental health crisis after remote learning and COVID in this ever-changing world. Lani created *A-Z MINDFUL ME* a fun, interactive resource for kids, families and communities to playfully explore mindfulness through present moment awareness, while laying a foundation to connect, heal, and become more resilient.

Stay updated and connected at the authors website at www.a-zmindfulness.com.

ABOUT A-Z MINDFUL ME

"When I practice Awareness, my body is calm and my breath is slow and relaxed. I feel great and ready for anything because I am calm and aware. I practice after school and before homework." **-Mike, 4th grade**

"When I practice Imagine my thoughts are calm, happy, and relaxed because I am thinking positive and it puts a good image in my head." **-Mimi, 5th grade**

"I was in a classroom using A-Z Mindfulness techniques. It was great to see staff applying what they learned so quickly. Taking time to be mindful is so important for kids and adults." **—Ann, Elementary School Principal**

"As a school social worker for 20+ years, I fully endorse that every family use A-Z Mindful Me. Teaching these mindfulness strategies is not just good for you, it's good for all of us." **- David Temkin, School Social Worker**

"Everyone enjoyed! We've talked about "letting thoughts go" (Cloud) and use Bee Buzzing. Students continue to practice these techniques that are so pertinent to everyday life." **-Emily, Elementary School Social Worker**

"Students walked away knowing how to use these strategies. We implemented Ocean breathing and are using the same language in our daily dialogue to tap out distractions and put our energy into what we need to be focused on. Students enjoy practicing what they've learned and are able to utilize these skills." **-3rd grade teacher**

"Students learned valuable tools to help them deal with real life situations. We learned so many ways to stay focused and calm. Our favorite ones were Energy and Imagine." **—Bricker, 1st grade teacher**

"We love having A-Z Mindfulness at the library. I am blown away by how insightful the kids are, regardless of age (K-5) or experience. Students are able to share things they may not have been aware of before they started. It's great for them to be able to walk away with techniques they can practice at home when needed." **-Amanda Lopez, Youth Services Programming Specialist, Northbrook Public Library**

www.ingramcontent.com/pod-product-compliance
Lightning Source LLC
Chambersburg PA
CBHW061114070526
44583CB00027B/3286